Copperhead

By Victoria Braidich

Gareth Stevens
Publishing

Please visit our website, www.garethstevens.com. For a free color catalog of all our high-quality books, call toll free 1-800-542-2595 or fax 1-877-542-2596.

Library of Congress Cataloging-in-Publication Data

Braidich, Victoria.
 Copperhead / Victoria Braidich.
     p. cm. — (Killer snakes)
 Includes index.
 ISBN 978-1-4339-5629-4 (pbk.)
 ISBN 978-1-4339-5630-0 (6-pack)
 ISBN 978-1-4339-5627-0 (library binding)
 1. Copperhead—Juvenile literature. I. Title.
 QL666.O69B73 2011
 597.96'3—dc22

                                    2010045997

First Edition

Published in 2012 by
Gareth Stevens Publishing
111 East 14th Street, Suite 349
New York, NY 10003

Copyright © 2012 Gareth Stevens Publishing

Designer: Michael J. Flynn
Editor: Greg Roza

Photo credits: Cover, pp. 1, (pp. 2–4, 6, 8–10, 12, 14, 16, 18, 20–24 snake skin texture), 5, 8–9, 13, 15, 19, 21 Shutterstock.com; pp. 7, 11 iStockphoto.com; p. 17 Jim Merli/Visuals Unlimited/Getty Images.

Printed in the United States of America

CPSIA compliance information: Batch #CS11GS: For further information contact Gareth Stevens, New York, New York at 1-800-542-2595.

Contents

Boldface words appear in the glossary.

Meet the Copperhead

The copperhead is the most common **venomous** snake in the eastern and central United States. It lives as far north as Massachusetts and as far west as Texas. It's called the North American copperhead because there are snakes called copperheads in other countries.

5

What Do They Look Like?

The heads of most copperhead snakes have a reddish-brown, or copper, color. This is how the snake got its name. Their heads are arrow shaped, too. Copperheads' bodies are tan or pinkish tan with brown bands. Young copperheads have a greenish or yellowish tail.

7

Most copperheads are between 24 and 36 inches (61 and 91 cm) long. However, some can grow to about 48 inches (122 cm) long. They weigh between 0.5 and 0.75 pound (0.23 and 0.34 kg). Female copperheads are commonly longer than males.

At Home with Copperheads

Copperheads can be found in many **habitats**, but they like areas with trees and water. They use their colors to hide in tall grass, bushes, dead trees, and rocks. Some people have found copperheads in their backyards!

11

Baby Copperheads

Female copperheads have 3 to 10 baby snakes once a year. Babies are about 10 inches (25 cm) long. They weigh less than an ounce (28 g). Female copperheads don't take care of their babies. The babies start hunting for bugs to eat right away.

Hide, or Bite?

When copperheads are afraid, they stop moving and wait for the danger to go away. Their colors help them hide in dead leaves and rocks. If they can't find a place to hide, they bite! Copperhead venom is strong enough to kill a small dog.

15

Silent Hunter

The copperhead also uses its colors to hide when hunting for **prey**. It has parts on its face called pits, which sense the heat of passing prey. Young copperheads use their brightly colored tails to **lure** prey, but adult copperheads don't need a lure.

Copperheads mainly like to eat mice. However, they also eat small birds, lizards, small snakes, frogs, bugs, and other small animals. The copperhead **attacks** its prey quickly and holds on to it with its **fangs** until its venom kills the small animal. Then the copperhead eats its prey whole!

19

People and Copperheads

More Americans are bitten by copperheads each year than by any other venomous snake! People don't usually die from copperhead bites, but the bites are very painful. If you ever see a copperhead, it's best to stay far away.

Snake Facts
Copperhead

Length	between 24 and 36 inches (61 and 91 cm); some grow to about 48 inches (122 cm)
Weight	0.5 to 0.75 pound (0.23 to 0.34 kg)
Where It Lives	eastern and central United States
Life Span	up to 20 years
Killer Fact	Copperheads use their fangs to shoot venom into their prey. If a copperhead loses a fang, another one grows in its place!

Glossary

attack: to try to harm someone or something

fang: a long, pointed tooth

habitat: the place in which an animal lives

lure: to trick an animal into getting close enough to catch it

prey: an animal hunted by other animals for food

venomous: able to produce a liquid called venom that is harmful to other animals

For More Information

Books

Gunderson, Megan M. *Copperheads*. Edina, MN: ABDO Publishing, 2011.

Mattern, Joanne. *Copperheads*. Mankato, MN: Capstone Press, 2009.

Websites

Copperhead Fact Sheet

nationalzoo.si.edu/Animals/ReptilesAmphibians/Facts/FactSheets/Northerncopperhead.cfm
Read more about the copperhead snake.

Pictures of American Copperhead Snakes

www.tigerhomes.org/animal/pictures-american-copperhead.cfm
See pictures of copperhead snakes from around the country.

Index